THE MOTHER SELF

THE MOTHER SELF

POEMS

Talia Gutin

Published: 2025
Printed in the United States of America
Print ISBN: 978-1-64742-895-2
E-ISBN: 978-1-64742-896-9
Library of Congress Control Number: 2025900940

For information, address:
She Writes Press
1569 Solano Ave #546
Berkeley, CA 94707

Interior Design by Kiran Spees

She Writes Press is a division of SparkPoint Studio, LLC.

For

My son, Jonah Moon—I will behold
and ponder you forever.

CONTENTS

DAY ONE

He was placed on my chest,
my whole world changed.

THE MOTHER

A return
to interior.

My body,
like my heart,
softens.

Remember
time's tenderness,
I straddle
joy and sorrow.

Holding him
feels holy.

YOU BECOME MY WORLD

I find
puddles
of breast milk
on my clothes
mattress
pillows
floor—
splashes of you
all over my world.

My darling,
the smell of your skin
(and I avow the lilacs
of spring are no sweeter)

opens me
into now
and here—

As I enter
irrevocably further
into a love severe,
into my own heart.

TO CONTAIN TIME

You, asleep
in my arms

as I drink this
exquisite peace—

My baby, please,
slow down.

DAY 25

As we bathed today, I held you against my skin in the water, and it felt like we were one body once more.

THE LOVER SETS THE BELOVED FREE:
Ghazal for a New Mother

I waver between worlds, holding tight and letting go,
Grasping and grieving each day, releasing and letting go.

It slips like silk through my fingertips—what is dearer than time?
Slow down, notice, and practice here, letting go.

I cradle him today and miss him for the moments we will part—
This love transforms then terrifies, and I fear letting go.

The sacred is a secret known only by the heart,
Why must I rush through life each year, never letting go?

My father said love's essence is this simple truth:
The lover sets the beloved free beyond the sphere of letting go.

HAVE YOU NOTICED?

Have you noticed what he loves to do?
How his eyes gleam in the silvery air?
Rippling ponds of blue surrounded by white clouds
in wonder of the trees, grass, and sky—
Did you see how he couldn't look away?
How he smiled at a bird's sudden landing atop a little branch—
as though perfectly designed, waiting all its life
to hold the weight of the winged animal?
And did you see how the sun thanked his rosy cheeks,
which warmed the sun and not the reverse?
And could you feel it, in your heart, the reverence of a child?
And have you, too, figured out what these moments are for?
And are you missing your life?

LEARNING HIS MAMA

Like a little stream,
gentle,

uncomplicated—

his finger traces
my face—

and my eyelashes,
cheekbones, lips—

stopping nowhere,
missing nothing.

DAY 38

Lying in bed this morning, I watched him sleep,
beholding who he is today.

THE FIRST BORN

These drifting days
are beautiful—

At home,
doing nothing,
being everything

with him,
my son.

THE INFINITE SILHOUETTE OF A MOTHER AND CHILD

Can the structure
of a woman's body become
whole as she holds her child?

How many women over
how many millennia have held
their infants as I do now?

Sensing your breath,
feathers on my skin,
my heart, too.

I untangle your tiny
fingers from my hair,
and place you into the crib—

At once, I feel
the absence of your form,
relearning the distant
wholeness of my own body.

HE CANNOT BE CONTROLLED

I learn

again &

again &

infinitely—

mothering is not

possession.

DAY 46

Today, we played in the grass, though your head
continuously lifted to the sky—your eyes, not with me,
but with those bluebirds.

HOW QUIET?

How quiet must I be
to witness the stars
serenade the moon?

How still must I become
to hear a ladybug flutter
its wings to fly?

And if I wish to hear the drumming
of his breath through the night,
I mustn't let out a peep at all.

WHEN HE LAUGHS

Not a choir of birds delighted
and dancing at dawn, or the silky
stir of the wind threading
its fingers through the pines;
neither those silent, brilliant
blossoms of May—

Could rival in sweetness, purity,
the music of his laughter—

Guttural giggles burst
from squinted eyes,
a toothless smile spreads
irrepressibly.

He pays no thought to why he laughs—
joy's pulsation, uninterrupted.

RECOGNIZING YOU

1.

I ask,

how many lifetimes
have we traveled together?

How many more to come?

2.

Three years later, he answers,

So many.

UNRAVELING

Into my chest, a small hand presses.
My whole body becomes
the imprint his palm expresses.
Where he exists, I exist; ego succumbs.

Nursing him, our eyes connect—
again, two bodies merge.
From these wells, I did not expect
such a love could surge.

Yet my unraveling identity
yearns for solid earth, my own.
Have I reached capacity?
Will I ever be alone?

My breath is not more vital than he,
but in loving him, I've lost parts of me.

THE TRUTH OF A MOTHER

Every night, I practice
releasing you,

every night, it hurts.

A REVIVAL

I.

Motherhood is a revival of being
from the diversion of doing—

Where you listen to what calls within,
sometimes sorrow, grief, despair—

and find the roots from which beauty grows.

2.

I am learning to pay attention—

When he discovered the sand,
his palms coated in granular stones, confounded
by the texture's novelty as he licked his fingers.

When I softly sway him in the night,
wreathed in darkness as the world slips away,
giving a sense of eternity.

How nature intended my shoulder
to be the perfect shape around which his hand
could grasp the crest of its blade.

When I whisper songs and prayers, not of religion
but devotion, echoing through his ears, rooting
in his heart.

Or as I lay him in the crib, his whole hand wrapping
around my two fingers as if to say:
Mama, are you still there? Mama, please stay.

3.

If these times lived unseen,
what, in this life, did I live for?

4.

And of such moments,
I think of Mary Oliver
when she wrote:

They could mean something.
They could mean everything.

DAY 55

You refused to go down for a nap today, and though maddening, I sourced unprecedented patience. It was a hard day. I hope tomorrow will be different.

DEAR SON

My heart loves flowers,
poetry, the moon—now you,
my son, my dear sun.

ALONE NOW

The hum of the wind floats
through the open window

carrying the chatter of birds
from a faraway branch—

silence of the late afternoon,
eyelids descend

my weary body collapses
on warm, white sheets

SOMETHING MY GRANDFATHER SAID TO ME
(that my bones now know)

If my love for you

were measured in distances,

there would be no end.

WHAT ELSE IS THERE?

Tell me, what is more important—

His body wraps
my chest,
alive to the tips
of his curled fingers,
no heavier than air,
resting on my collarbone.

Tell me, eager mind,
possessed by
productivity—

What do you fear?

This life slips by,
these days will
disappear.

HOW HE LOVES ME

From time to time
I catch him staring,
his eyes seeming to say:

Look at her,
look at my mama.

DAY 64

I woke up this morning with a painful breast infection. Though struggling, this truth shakes my core: there is nothing, ever, I would not endure for you.

TWO THINGS

that so effortlessly catch attention,

the flames of a campfire—
dancing skyward
at once elegant and feral,

the infallibility of an infant
merely and miraculously existing—

how is it, sweet one, that you are here?

WILD

Lying in bed,
	our limbs entangled
like wild vines—
	mother and son
yoking.

THE WRITER IS THE ONE WHO WITNESSES THEIR WORLD

Where some look to

society, culture, politics,
I look to the crescent moon

anchored in that black abyss,
in no rush at all.

MONDAY MORNING

Still dark,
dreams unresolved.

Whimpers reverberate
in the air,

Mama

  Mama

   Mama

I spring out of bed
and lift your warm body—

your messy hair
smells of sweat
and orange blossoms.

As is so
every morning,
I am fervent and swollen
with love.

That, somehow,
you are mine,

that, somehow,
and already,

you are yours.

UNFURLING

Am I unfurling as the ferns do in springtime?
Coiled into themselves, demure—
then awakening with profound intelligence,
to the sun, the warming earth,
expressing their leaves, opening to the forest—

Is it brave, or is nature simply doing what she does?
Am I brave?

Nonetheless, I wonder: Do the ferns feel pain
in this transfiguration?

DAY 76

On our walk through Prospect Park tonight, you never stopped smiling at me from your stroller. The wind and sky were beautiful, and you, my child, were beautiful. I cherish these moments most of all.

A REFLECTION ON BEING

To experience yourself—

an unceasing experiment of revelation,
of unearthing and becoming,
unbecoming, too.

More parts always and patiently unfold—
And above all, to live in accordance
with your heart.

Some years are for questing,
some are for answers.

What question calls you now?
And now?
Are you listening?

A PROMISE

May I open to your smile
always,
anywhere—

May it press against my chest,
carry me into delight
and that indelible ache
of love.

Today, two small teeth
encircled by tender gums.

How will it look
when you are five?
Ten? Thirty?

When, perhaps one day, I gaze upon you,
gazing upon your own child?

NOTES FROM A RARE MORNING OF SOLITUDE

I.

Flower buds,
like drops of blood, drip
from the branches,
reviving the oak trees
from a solemn winter.

2.

Meandering, I notice
a bouquet of purple petals,
ripening above the curved path—

This spring, it feels like the world
is being created all over again.

That the sea of leaves
sings in generosity:

may we begin anew.

3.

If you never know who you are in aloneness
you will only know your loneliness.

4.

I don't know what God is.
Though I have known the presence of something

great, perhaps unexplainable,
when I have sat in still, impenetrable solitude.

A nearby tree is always helpful.
And the grass, warm as a rug, on bare feet.

5.

If perfectionism and achievement
no longer drove you, what would?

IN THE GRASS

You sit twirling a blade of grass,
marveling at the novelty of it all—
the world.

I sit, too, marveling
at the novelty of you.

DAY 82

We wandered together along the Montauk shore this evening. The breeze, grounding and enchanting, like the setting sun, burrowed behind the clouds. The sea sang like a bird, soaring into the looming stars.

I AM YOUR MOTHER

What do you need, my darling?

To be embraced
as the sun to the sea,
faithfully?

Each morning, stretching
her limbs upon that blue mystery—

The sea knowing, undoubtedly,
tomorrow, she will return.

Are you after more play and laughter?
Then I will sit with you, forever,
making silly faces.

Or let us delight through the woods,
greeting the ferns and goldfinches—
after all, it is springtime.

Or is my presence what you prefer?

>

By which I mean,
being with you,
nothing more—

I am here.
I will always be here.
I am your mother.

TO MY MOTHER

I could not know then
what I know now,

the willingness
to die for someone

to never have a greater
reason to live—

how serious a thing it is,
a mother's love.

THE WORLD WAS HAPPENING

Minutes ago, fresh cotton sheets—
onto which he stood
and smiled
and collapsed
and stood
and smiled
and collapsed
and stared—

Into pools of pale blue, I stared back.

Meanwhile, the world was happening.
Meanwhile, nothing had ever felt so important.

THE MOTHER BIRD

I.

On my daily walk through the wooded path, I spot
   a bird's nest—
a golden wreath wedged and camouflaged in slender
tree branches, stitched with sticks, leaves, grass,
and whatever else holds these marvelous structures together.

Four or five fuzzy, mostly bald heads bobble in unison,
pointy beaks involuntarily gaped,
each like an orchid, deep and delicate.

They utter a raspy and desperate plea—
feed me, protect me, please don't leave.

I discover the mother scouting the other side of the path,
anticipating the threat of strangers—
a helpless worm dangles from her beak.

>

Questions of the Self do not occur to her;
Not once, I assume, does she consider
ambition or sacrifice.

Are you ever lonely, mother bird?

Some mornings, do you wake up sad?

Are you struck daily by a love so profound it terrifies you?

Mother bird, do you feel free?

2.

From time to time, I wonder
who and where I would be
without him,

who and where I was
before him—

3.

Still,

on the hardest days,

flooded with responsibility,
with feeling—

I choose this life with him.

4.

She follows her earthly role
with relentless purpose.

Something beyond the mother bird
guides her, dictating each decision and action.

This same intelligence lives within me,
as it does in the mother deer and the mother wolf.

5.

No linearity
in feeling

floating &
falling into

inner rivers
of being—

who decided
on this rational world?

6.

Mothering, how you draw or drag

those daring and those afraid into humility,

into beauty and pain's proximities,

into whatever the velveteen rabbit meant when it said:

Real isn't how you are made, it is a thing that happens to you.

7.

Weeks later, I returned to the tree,
the same straw-like structure intact.

I never saw the mother bird or hatchlings again.

INTO SELF

My husband left for work today,
and a wave of resentment
pulsed through my body—
perhaps envy.

He does not face
the daily struggle—

What do I choose?

If I stay, will I lose myself?
If I leave, will I lose part of my child?
If I do it all, will I drown?

He goes to work
and comes home.

I yearn for clarity,
knowing it is not found
in the world outside—

>

So further into myself
I go.

Day after day,
in my quietest hours,
I listen for those innermost
whispers of wisdom,

which only I
may hear,

which only I
may live.

I WANT TO STAY, I WANT TO LEAVE

This afternoon, your cheek
on my collarbone,
bleary eyes face mine—

I kiss your lips,
and you giggle,

I kiss you again
and a few more times,
never wanting to stop.

But I do,
and place you in the crib
for your naptime,

my solitude.

RED LEAF

Hidden
in the tall
grass, it glistens red.

I halt to peer closer at the bloody hue
and its web of yellow veins. Bits of its lacy
body are ripped or rotted, browned edges
curl up and in.

In death, as in life,
the leaf holds beauty.

And who could argue its fall as any less important
or intelligent as its bloom?
Both in humility and grace.

Dusk looms as I tuck the leaf into my pocket,
and the day yields to warm darkness.

SOLITUDE

Chosen time alone,
to learn who you are
and who you are not.

Allow patience in your pace,
trust in time's intelligence,
revive your soul.

Sink into silence as you dissolve
into the immense, unspeakable
mystery.

"I FELT FREE AND THEREFORE I WAS FREE"
—Jack Kerouac

I traveled the world
when I was twenty-three,
in search of somewhere.

I paddled my kayak
along the Andaman Sea
and left it far from shore.
Then I leaped into the turquoise,
and swam beside pillars
of limestone, dripping
in green moss.

Minutes or hours later,
I flipped onto my back to stare
at those eternal ethers—

Then I knew.

Then everything became everything else.

I was the sea and the cliffs,
the fish and the powdery
puddles of the sky—

and I lingered there,
perfectly glad.

What else should I have done?

LOSING AND FINDING

I.

Sometimes
loving you
is lonely.

2.

Sometimes
the lonelier I feel,
the more I pull away—

not from you,
but the world &

me.

3.

Where

             is

                        my

center

             now,

having

                                been

                           swept

                                away

                in

            you?

4.

In loneliness,
have we forgotten
ourselves?

5.

How disorienting

       to feel

simultaneously

       displaced

and

       like the most

natural me

       I've ever

known.

6.

Connected with Self, we are never alone—
finding company in the rivers, trees,
and those bright and silent ladybugs.

7.

Will I ever arrive
closer to life's clear center
than with you, my child?

IT WON'T BE LONG

A difficult step up the park hill,
where he has never walked,
every inch of earth, a revelation.

Without hesitation, he reaches
for my hand: *Will you help, Mama?*

Then time whispers,
There will be a day
he stops reaching for you.

A MEDITATION

Tomorrow,

I will bathe in pearls of dew spilling
from the grass—

which I've heard
are kisses from God—

as the sun cradles me
in her palms.

AN ORDINARY AFTERNOON

Removed from being seen,
the more richly I see—

when restlessness recedes
and envy for something

or anything evaporates
like puddles in August heat.

What remains is the soul of the earth,
and the roots of this human life.

By that, I mean ordinary,
unsophisticated moments,

Where reverence
dwells.

I SEE IT NOW

Five years old,

your first day of kindergarten,

a little hand slipping out of mine,

leaving—

Thirteen,

your voice begins to change,

the way I see you

changes, too—

Eighteen,

and off to college,

I come home—

the emptiness of your bedroom.

Still, for now,

you are twelve days old.

Your fragile frame fits

exquisitely

into the crest

of my elbow—

You won't be forever,
but today, you are my baby.

DAY 100

I realized something today: I always knew I would look at you with absolute love—I did not know you would look at me that very same way.

STORY OF SELF

I.

I devoted years of life in search of my Self, traversing forests and mountains, grappling with countless philosophies, spiritual wisdom, and great literature— what I found always slipped away.

After giving birth, each day with my son felt dreamy and disorienting, the most real and absolute experience of my life. My identity, as I knew it, unraveled.

I grieved this loss.

From the six-year-old who never stopped yearning for my mother's nurturance; to the untethered twenty-three-year-old who traveled the world; to my marriage as it had been and could never return; to my loneliness and fear as life beckoned me into the next evolution of my womanhood; and to the resisted, inevitable acceptance that knew, each day, my child would grow older.

2.

Maybe the Self is not singular, but multiple; not fixed, but fluid. Like the waves of the sea, continuously unfolding, invariably changed by the storms and hidden currents of its inner and outer worlds.

In grief, the Self renews.

In grief, mothering becomes a conduit to the sacred— the very center and soul of this life.

What the rivers and birds have always known, that liminal space the moon invites us into night after night.

3.

In grief, I behold my son with awe.

AS LIFE WILL

I cannot tell you
      how
or when—
      I have been looking
all along—
      but somehow,
he became
      a little boy.

TO THE NEW MOTHER

If you sink
into this breathtaking storm

and stay
a little longer,

if you let it swallow you,
until you are swollen with feeling,

if you let it carry you
into darkness, and maybe alone—

For a little while,
you will not see,

you will find
no answers,

which, as Rilke said,
could not be given to you now

>

because you would not be able
to live them.

But I promise you—
the pain passes,

the loneliness
lifts.

Let this time be your temple,
your induction.

You will be wiser, sturdier,
immovable—

Your innermost Self
metamorphosed.

This is you waxing and waning
into wholeness.

—Me (two years later)

ABOUT THE AUTHOR

Talia Gutin is a writer, certified life coach (PCC), and mother. She received her master's degree from New York University, where she studied psychology and creative writing, combining her love of language with a deep curiosity for the human psyche. She is the lead coach at Mindful Marriage and Family Therapy, based in New York City, where she guides individuals and couples on their paths to emotional and mental wellness.

Talia lives in Boulder, Colorado, with her husband and two children. This is her debut collection of poetry.

Connect with Talia on social media @taliagutin and visit her website at www.taliagutin.com.

ACKNOWLEDGMENTS

I am deeply grateful to my family for their unwavering encouragement throughout my journey of writing this book. To my husband, Sam, and our beautiful children, Jonah and Nora—the home and love we share mean everything to me.

Thank you to She Writes Press for providing the support and platform to share my poems with the world. I am also indebted to New York University for the educational foundation and creative inspiration I received there. Thank you to my professors, Dave King and Allyson Paty, for their guidance in the earliest days when this book was just an idea.

To my editor, Cin Salach, whose keen insights and suggestions were invaluable in strengthening each poem—thank you.

Lastly, I wish to acknowledge the poets and writers who have inspired me, especially Mary Oliver and Rainer Maria Rilke. Your words are forever imprinted on my mind and soul.

NOTES

"Recognizing You": I added the second section three years after I wrote section one, inspired by a moment with my son. After listening to the poem, he simply responded, "So many." Incorporating his words naturally reflected our shared experience.

"A Revival": Section four includes two lines from Mary Oliver's "Invitation."

"Something My Grandfather Said to Me (that my bones now know)": In one of our last conversations, my grandfather, known for his logical and rational nature, expressed a sentiment that remains one of the most poetic I've ever heard: "If my love for you were measured in distances, there would be no end."

In other words (a phrase he often used), he told me: I love you, and infinitely.

"The Mother Bird": Section six references one of the most influential books of my childhood, *The Velveteen Rabbit*, by Margery Williams Bianco.

"Real isn't how you are made," said the Skin Horse. "It's a thing that happens to you. When a child loves you for a long, long time, not just to play with, but REALLY loves you, then you become Real."

"Does it hurt?" asked the Rabbit.

"Sometimes," said the Skin Horse, for he was always truthful. "When you are Real you don't mind being hurt."

"I Felt Free and Therefore I Was Free": The title comes from Jack Kerouac's *The Dharma Bums*.

"To the New Mother": Several lines in this poem are drawn from Rainer Maria Rilke's *Letters to a Young Poet*. Rilke's emphasis on embracing solitude and seeking truth within oneself echoes throughout the pages of this book.

Looking for your next great read?

We can help!

Visit www.shewritespress.com/next-read
or scan the QR code below for a list
of our recommended titles.

She Writes Press is an award-winning
independent publishing company founded to
serve women writers everywhere.